MANUEL CADRECHA PERKINS+WILL

CONTENTS

I THINK OF BUILDINGS AS COMPLETE FORMS,
NOT AS ASSEMBLIES OF PIECES. I IMAGINE
THE BUILDING, THEN I DRAW WHAT I IMAGINE.
THE BUILDING SPRINGS FROM AN IDEA.

DESIGN WITH EMPATHY AND EXPERIENCE

PHIL HARRISON, FAIA
CEO, PERKINS+WILL

ARCHITECTURE IS AN ART OF SYNTHESIS.
Our work is to consider, balance, and integrate science and art—tectonics, function, and fabrication, but also form, volume, light, and materiality. Architects do this as a matter of course, but exceptional architects do more.

Beyond science and art, inspired design is realized more rarely and emerges from a broad consideration of experience—our emotional response to environments, the context of human history, interpersonal behavior and interaction, the expectation for change over time, the convergence of human occupation with our natural environment, and a multitude of other possibilities. Exceptional architects, therefore, must be deeply empathetic polymaths, and Manuel Cadrecha is precisely this.

Cadrecha's work is marked by who he is as a person—someone with a global education and experience, combined with tremendous agility, curiosity, and humility. This rare combination allows Cadrecha to understand, adapt, and thrive in virtually any circumstance, with all types of clients or collaborators. In a world where accomplished architects tend towards arrogance, Cadrecha is uncommonly empathetic.

Armed with this broad experience and deeply humane capacity, Cadrecha is able to reach more complex levels of design synthesis in a natural and unforced manner. For example, his work embraces the integration of multiple design scales—strategy, urban context, site, building, interior, and graphic design. At a macro scale, he adeptly translates learnings between projects, typologies, and cultures, resulting in an even more remarkable level of design synthesis. Ultimately, this is a form of creative optimism.

Cadrecha's curiosity and joyful spirit push him to find opportunity in everything, and, as a result, he has continuously grown as a design professional. I can say this because he and I have worked side by side for 21 years. Indeed, we have become great friends over these years, working together on numerous projects, and sharing (and even cooking) many great meals. He has had a positive impact on me, on his many collaborators, and our entire firm.

This book is testament to the power of empathy and experience. Please enjoy it.

THE LAST HUMANIST PROFESSION

MY FATHER WAS AN ENGINEER.
When I was growing up, he instilled in me an admiration for ancient Rome: its civilization, culture, and design. When I decided to become an architect, my father was delighted because he believed that architecture is the last humanist profession. Looking back on my career, I agree with him.

I can trace my first interest in architecture to 1964 when, while living in New York, I visited the World's Fair. The futuristic pavilions and overwhelming sense of progress excited me; it was just around the corner. I marveled at the Unisphere, the fair's iconic stainless steel earth sculpture. The fair was about the future and about a convergence of global cultures. My father, who was born in Spain, took me to the Spanish Pavilion. I remember being amazed at seeing one of El Cid's swords. I also became interested in the sense of my own heritage in an old and mysterious culture.

MY YOUTH, SPENT IN BOTH THE OLD
AND NEW WORLDS, SHAPED MY
WORK AND VIEW OF THE WORLD.

We moved to Madrid two years later. It was quite a change. I remember going with my mother to a palace-like bank where she filled out forms with pens that needed to be dipped in ink. I walked to stores, museums, cafés, and friends' houses. I rode trolley cars and watched with fascination as the driver with a single-lever control guided the car on its tracks through park lanes, neighborhoods, and boulevards. I admired the beautiful scale and details of the buildings and everyday life. Madrid instilled a love for history and tradition deep within me, as well as a belief of art's ability to elevate our existence.

Going back to New York for my senior year of high school, I remember standing in ticket lines on bright summer days in Central Park. I stood amongst the grass and trees outside Joe Papp's Shakespeare in the Park, a brooding, self-concerned young Hamlet with an uncertain future in front of me. Looking beyond the trees, I was delighted by

the fantastic array of the tall ribbon of buildings bordering the park. They were varied in height, form, age, and style. They were elegant and optimistic and owned their place in the city. New York charged me with a passion for modernity, as well as the power of creative invention to improve our lives.

My youth, spent in both the old and new worlds, shaped my work and view of the world. As an architect, I feel strongly that buildings should be culturally relevant, historically aware, forward-looking, adaptable, and most importantly, beautiful.

In architecture, I feel a deep connection to my past and my future, to tradition and innovation, and to beauty and invention. I love being an architect because, in architecture, I can have the remarkable effect of improving people's lives and bridging cultures together.

DESIGN FOR
COLLABORATION

1315 PEACHTREE STREET
ATLANTA, GEORGIA

WHEN MY DAUGHTERS WERE LITTLE, my wife and I would bring them to the library in this concrete building on Peachtree Street. They loved that the library was on the second floor, with large windows overlooking the High Museum of Art and the graceful treetops of the adjacent neighborhood.

Years later, Perkins+Will purchased the building and I had the distinct pleasure of working with many of the firm's most talented designers to transform it into a model for urban regeneration. It is now among the most energy efficient buildings in the world, a first-class creative design workplace, a home for a museum dedicated to design, and a library to inspire future generations.

I hope to one day bring my grandchildren.

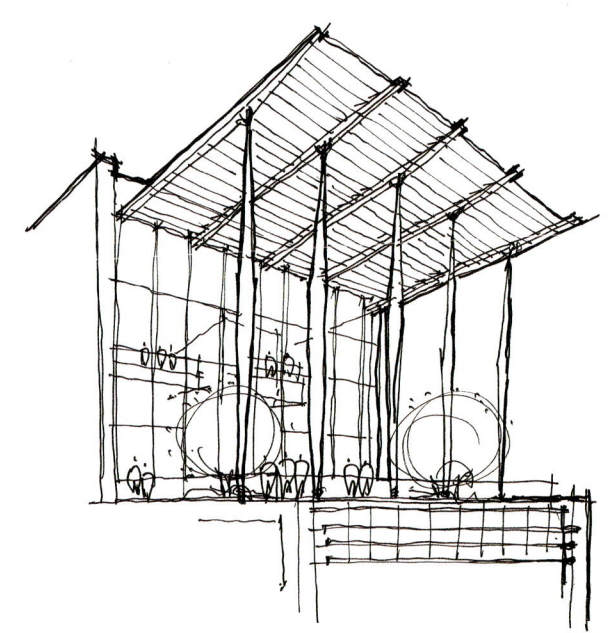

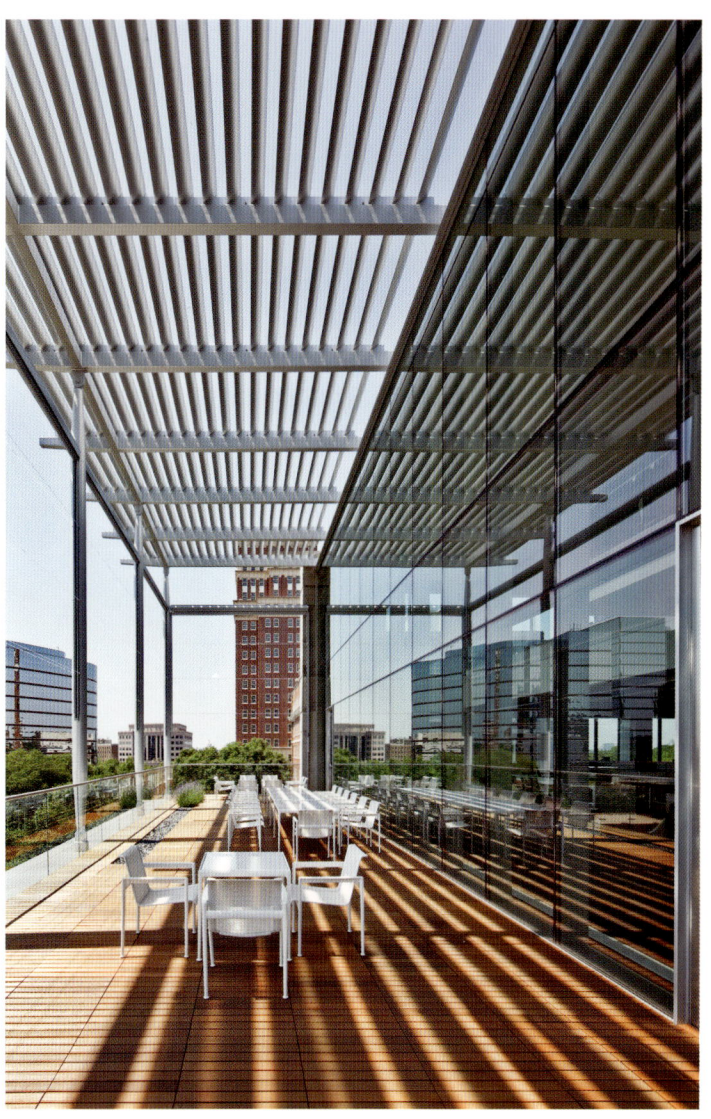

Open plan, open air.

Rainwater is harvested and reused throughout the site.

Transparency means open systems
and ideas on display.

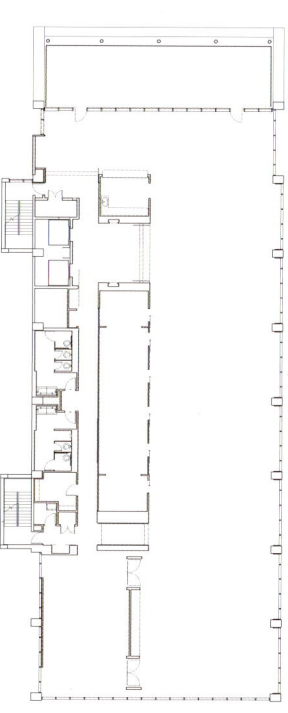

Floor plan

SANY AMERICA EXECUTIVE HEADQUARTERS AND ASSEMBLY PLANT

PEACHTREE CITY, GEORGIA

I HAVE BEEN WORKING ON PROJECTS in China since 2007. It was interesting to me that I would have the opportunity to work for one of my first Chinese clients on a manufacturing building in rural Georgia, forty minutes south of my home in Atlanta.

This project is the first USA-located manufacturing facility for SANY, a major Chinese heavy construction equipment company. Having prepared multiple master plans for SANY in China, Germany, and Brazil, our team was familiar with the company's insistence on high performance and iconic design.

We studied SANY and its processes, as well as Albert Kahn and his magnificent industrial buildings of the early 20th century. Our design is a clear span, sky-lit, open manufacturing space elegantly and simply enclosed in a modern, kit-of-parts assembly that support the manufacturing ethos of the SANY organization. A three-story, silicone-glazed, north-facing glass wall fully reveals the internal production process, while a modern, machine-aesthetic form encompasses the entry lobby and office areas.

Sitting in rural Georgia, this project has an unexpected sculptural presence. I love its simplicity.

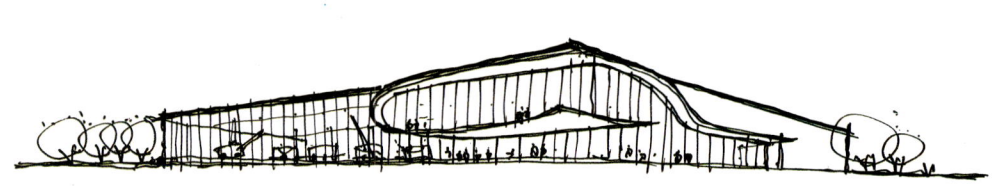

Chinese high tech in rural Georgia.

DARDEN RESTAURANTS SUPPORT CENTER

ORLANDO, FLORIDA

I LOVE TO COOK. I COOK EVERY DAY.
It's a great sense of alchemy, like magic, bringing together diverse ingredients to create a delicious meal. I loved working for Darden because it was all about food and people who care about food.

Darden Restaurants, based in Orlando, Florida is the largest full service restaurant company in the world. With the design of their new restaurant support center, Darden wished to create a unifying culture combining their chains including Olive Garden, LongHorn Steakhouse, and Red Lobster under the same roof. This project is about making a place for cross-brand collaboration, for restaurant professionals to work together and learn from each other, to develop recipes, and to form a creative culinary community.

We worked closely with the executives, staff, and chefs to create a building and site design that supports this kind of collaboration. In order to accomplish this, our design team— including architects, interior designers, brand specialists, and landscape architects—had to demonstrate the same interdisciplinary values. With this approach, my role as design director was not so different from that of a chef, balancing flavors and talent to deliver an unforgettable meal. The resulting restaurant support center brings diverse creative people together in a vibrant place filled with the history and spirit of Darden.

My wife and I were redesigning our kitchen at the same time as I was working on this project. I received invaluable advice from the Darden Chefs on the appliances and new cookware!

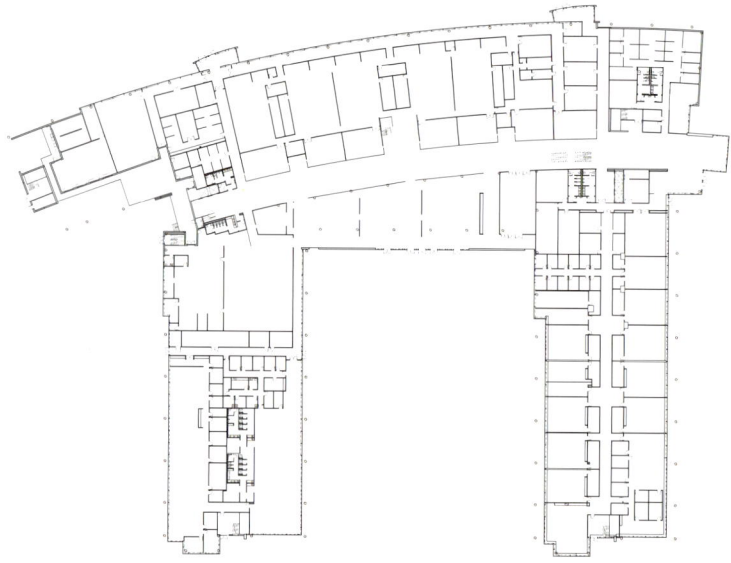

Floor plan

Celebrating food. Celebrating history.

Colorful and active.

Quiet and tailored.

BOSPHORUS TOWER

ISTANBUL, TURKEY

DRAWING INSPIRATION FROM
the beautiful lapping waters of the
Bosphorus Strait, the Bosphorus
Tower attempts to capture the romance
of Istanbul, a historic and modern
metropolis. I love this city, its generous
and hospitable people, its magnificent
history as a strategic connection
between Europe and Asia, and its
incredible vibrancy and continued
relevance as a center for business and
commerce.

A dramatic addition to the skyline, we
also designed the tower to connect to
the neighborhood with a sculptural retail
pavilion, entry courtyard, and plaza,
which create public spaces for people to
gather. The tower is elevated from the
entry courtyard, creating an expansive
entryway, with sleek floor-to-ceiling
walls that provide views to a fountain in
the internal plaza.

The position for the tower allows not
only views of the Bosphorus Strait, but
Istanbul's entire historic city center.
The rooftop terrace allows for sweeping
views of the city, the water, and Asia.

We designed the glass curtainwall of
the tower in rhythmic vertical sheets
that recall the glistening waters of the
Bosphorus. Quietly dramatic, this tower
is an attempt to reconcile modernity
with historic place.

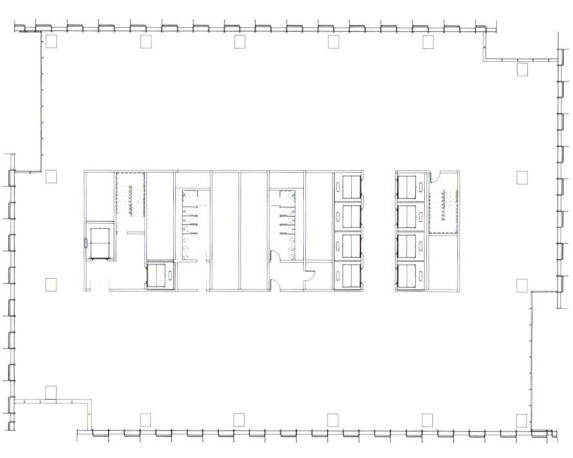

Floor plan

DESIGN FOR
WELLNESS

MAYO CLINIC HOSPITAL

JACKSONVILLE, FLORIDA

OUR CLIENT FOR THE MAYO CLINIC

Hospital told me early on, "Mayo is about evolution, not revolution." We took these words to heart.

Our team was tasked with adding the first inpatient hospital building to the verdant campus of the Mayo Clinic in Jacksonville, Florida. During on-site and off-site design sessions exploring countless planning, architectural, and interior design schemes, we always opted to carry forward the cleanest, most direct, and most Mayo-specific ideas.

With a site deep in the campus, the hospital entrance needed to be visible and inviting. As a world class health provider, the building needed to convey a quiet elegance and confidence. Our solution was a three-story loggia, which became the single most pronounced architectural element of the project.

The composition of the architecture is rigorous, clear, and straightforward; the detailing is careful, inventive, and confident. The material palette is a continuation and refinement of the existing materials. The interiors are equally restrained and assured.

I spent years working with this project, this team, and this client, distilling ideas to their essence, relating always to the Mayo Way. I consider it to be one of my best projects.

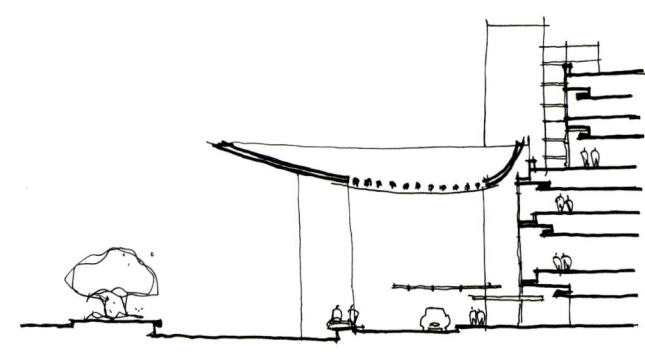

Materials, patterns, and light
in a restorative setting.

Dale Chihuly sculpture in the lobby.

DUKE MEDICINE PAVILION
DURHAM, NORTH CAROLINA

MY DAUGHTER WENT TO UNC CHAPEL Hill, so my passion for this project, at rival Duke University, has at times—jokingly—been a subject of family arguments.

The Duke Medicine Pavilion sits at the heart of the Duke University Medical Center. Our approach to the architectural design is conscious of and makes significant references to the iconic neo-gothic character of the Duke academic campus. Clearly, we did this in a modern vocabulary—developing an intricacy of detail, varied scales, and organizational compositions relevant to the source material. The architecture supports a "high-tech, high-touch" environment, consistent with the hospital's innovative mission.

The design was conceived as the front door and centerpiece of a district of new clinical facilities, including a major cancer center and nursing building that overlook a magnificent park designed by Laurie Olin. A generous plaza welcomes patients and visitors and connects the three surrounding buildings with graceful, calming, and accessible outdoor spaces.

The innovative floor planning at the Duke Medicine Pavilion creates an inward-looking environment focused around elevated open courtyards and gardens in order to maximize the access to natural light and improve the speed of patient recovery. Open vistas to the academic campus heighten the sense of place and identity.

Our large and talented team of architects, landscape architects, interior designers, and brand specialists worked over many years with a hands-on client to meet Duke University's high standards for design excellence.

As it turns out, my other daughter's fiancée went to Duke and he is happy with the design. The rivalry lives on.

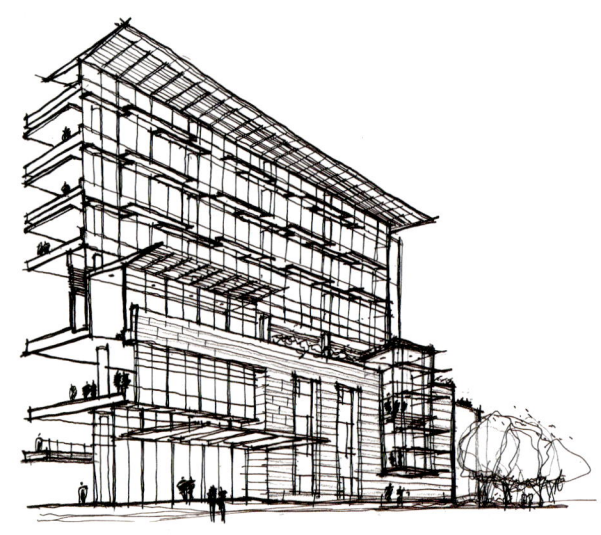

Careful detailing and use of materials provide quiet interest, variety, and echoes of Duke's history.

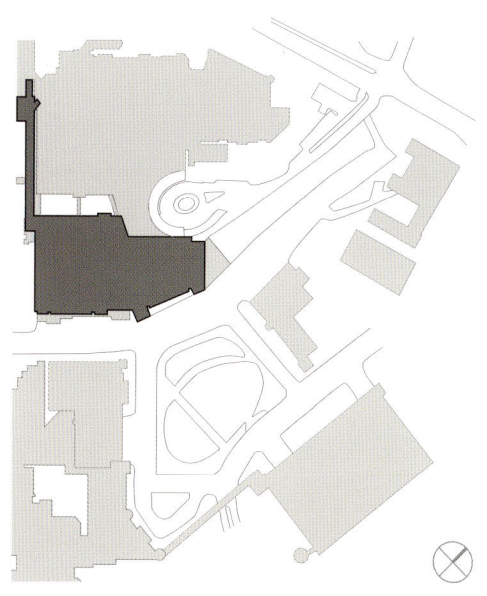

Site plan

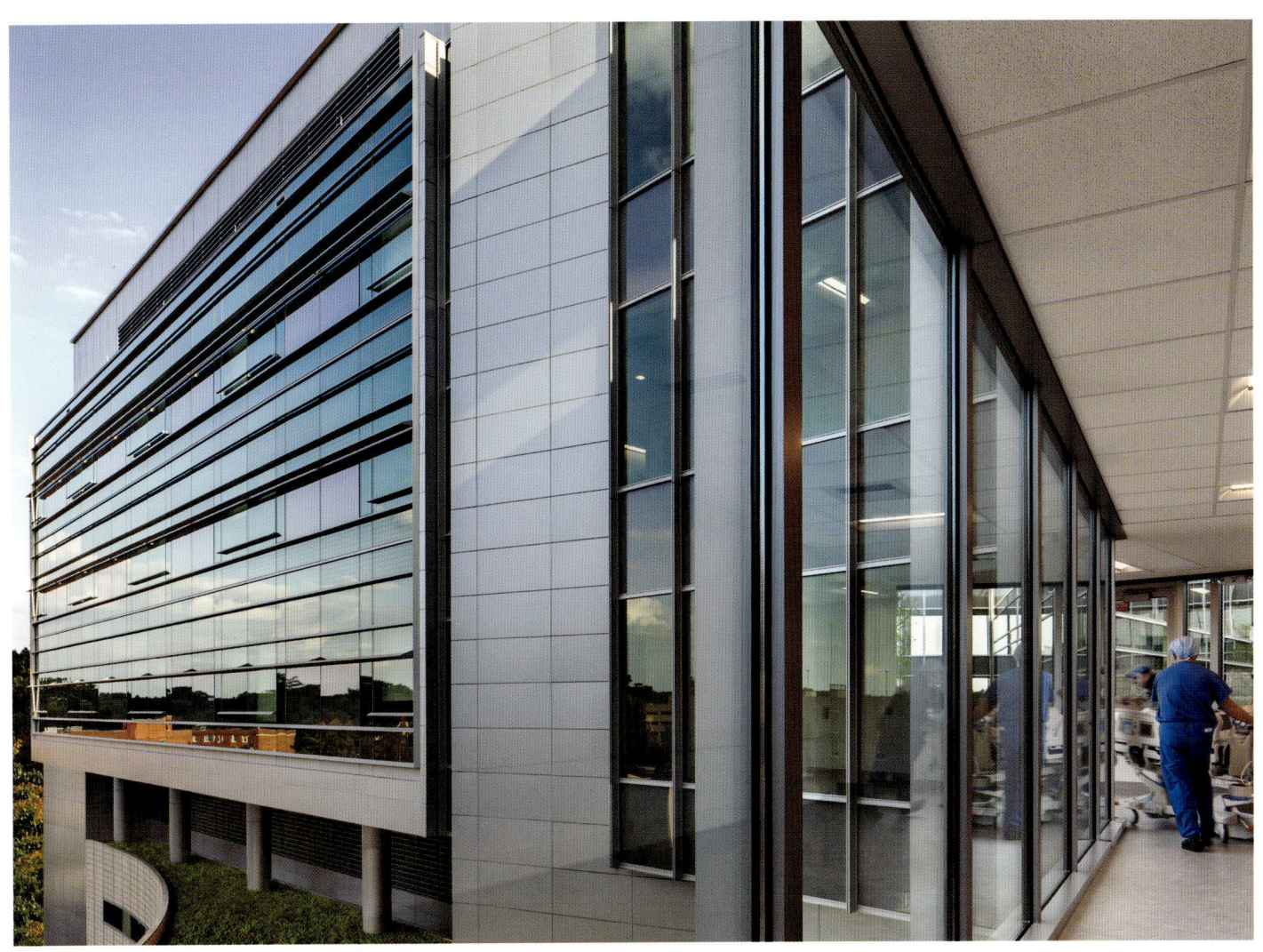

DESIGN FOR
LEARNING

RICHLAND COLLEGE, SABINE HALL SCIENCE BUILDING

DALLAS, TEXAS

NOT ALL BUILDINGS NEED TO STAND OUT.
Many buildings better serve their sites as good participants. This project is located on a college campus planned and designed by Perkins+Will more than thirty years ago and beautifully sited along a natural stream. This campus has withstood the "test of time" and continues to grow according to our original master plan concepts.

Our effort here was to work within the clear and successful parameters of the campus guidelines, finding natural opportunities to introduce new complimentary elements to the rich language.

Forward-looking at its core, the building is designed and built to LEED Platinum standards with systems and operations minimizing the campus's carbon footprint and its negative impact on the environment. In addition to a 43% energy reduction, consumption of potable water was reduced by 87%.

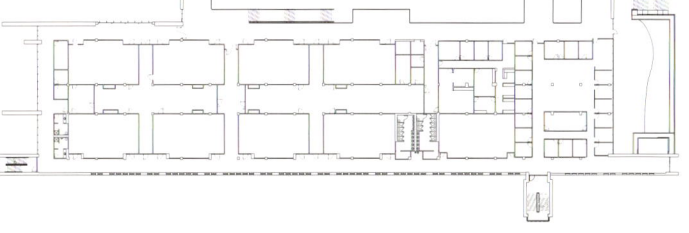

Floor plan

The beauty of shadows.

The beauty of light.

TEXAS A&M UNIVERSITY, INTERDISCIPLINARY LIFE SCIENCES BUILDING (ILSB)

COLLEGE STATION, TEXAS

TEXAS A&M IS AN INSTITUTION famously rich in tradition. Academic campuses often struggle with capturing the proper architectural expression of their heritage while embracing an image of innovation. This major project was the first project to use Texas A&M's new campus design guidelines.

The site was strategically located between the traditional and new campuses and significantly fronted the historic Simpson Drill Field. We viewed this large project as an opportunity to bridge the cultural divide and serve as a link for both the campus and the many disciplines that would use the building.

A broad limestone arcade forms an elegant porch along the side of the drill field and modulates the building volumes while providing a shaded place to observe the field. The building plan shape follows the established student pedestrian patterns, while the building's massing adjusts to compliment the height of existing buildings. This design strives to be a gentle, but direct architecture that is horizontal, modern, and at home with the heritage of this great institution. "Howdy."

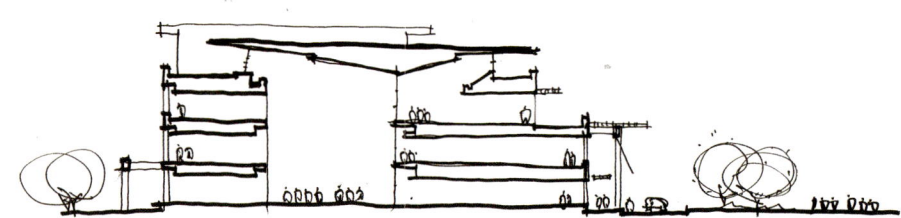

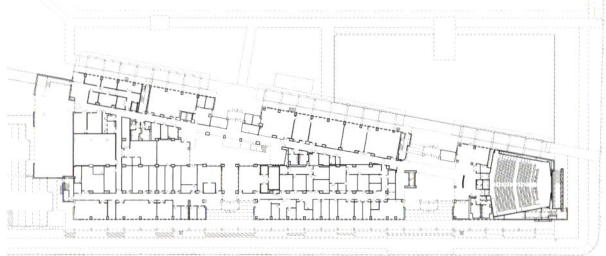

Floor plan

GEORGIA INSTITUTE OF TECHNOLOGY,
J. ERSKINE LOVE, JR. MANUFACTURING BUILDING

ATLANTA, GEORGIA

THIS WAS MY FIRST OPPORTUNITY
to design a building at my alma mater, Georgia Tech. The project is the third building in a suite of engineering buildings and serves to form an important interior edge to a shared open space. The site is at the traditional academic edge of the campus.

The building serves as the home for two distinct engineering departments at Georgia Tech, Mechanical Engineering and Material Science Engineering—they "break things."

The first two engineering buildings were fine designs by Terry Sargent. His buildings marked a departure from the historicist trend and the frequently bland contemporary strip window wallpaper buildings of campus buildings over the previous decades. His buildings were highly formed with strong, manufacturing-inspired detailing.

I saw Erskine Love as a compliment to Sargent's buildings and also as a bridge to Georgia Tech's fine mid-century modern buildings of the '40s and '50s. I saw this project as an opportunity to begin a path towards creating an architectural position that would reflect the innovative engineering character of this important research institution.

The composition is formed by two wings in an L shape that create an outdoor internal courtyard with the adjacent engineering building. The wings meet at a multistory study space that was voted by the students to be the favorite place to study on campus. I understand that the students took to referring to the building after a B-52s song, "Love Shack." With a clear planning diagram and an architectural composition that is expressive of program, the Erskine Love building is among my favorite projects.

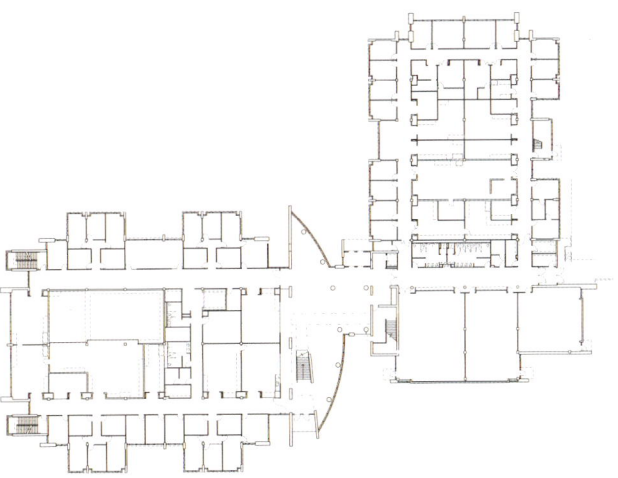

Floor plan

GEORGIA INSTITUTE OF TECHNOLOGY, CHRISTOPHER W. KLAUS ADVANCED COMPUTING BUILDING

ATLANTA, GEORGIA

IT'S DAUNTING TO DESIGN A BUILDING
at your own alma mater, but designing one directly next to your faculty, an international-style building by Paul Heffernan, with many of your ex-professors looking on expectantly, is frankly a bit intimidating. It was, however, great fun.

This major computer building is located directly next to the architecture school where I received my education. I quickly felt at home with the site and its location and shape enclosing a central open space with a broad arc that has earned the building's moniker "the colosseum of computing."

The team embraced our inner nerds and created a binary pattern system that establishes the building's brand and guides students along its elevated pathways. Streamlined tower forms allude to Georgia Tech's famous administration tower, and a glass surfboard stair landing harkens to the digital west coast.

Fun, expressive, and social, this building is well at home on the Tech campus and I hope a good neighbor to the architecture building. As an added bonus, the building served as the movie set for a fictional Google headquarters, where my daughter works. Lots of connections.

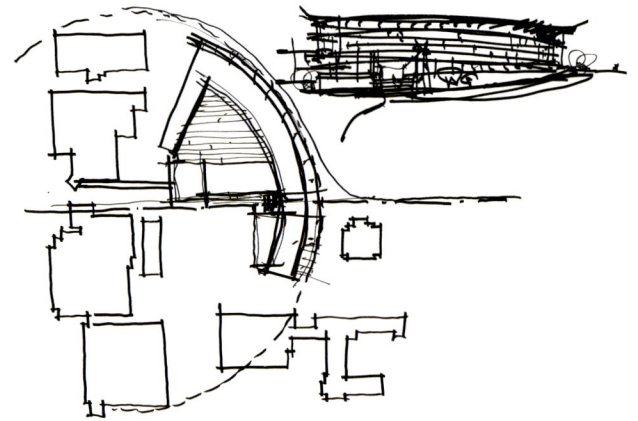

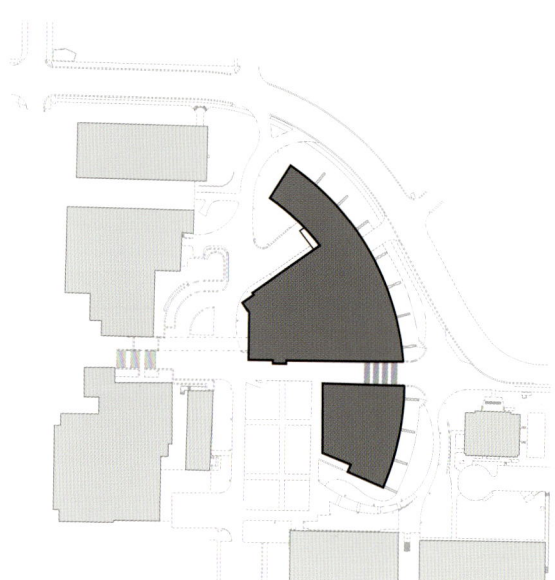

Site plan

BENJAMIN E. MAYS HIGH SCHOOL

ATLANTA, GEORGIA

THIS IS A TRANSFORMATION PROJECT.
The existing building was an interior-focused, closed, box-like structure—a very '70s building. There was little natural light, views, or a sense of visual inter-connectivity between classrooms and shared learning areas. Our approach was to build on the original idea of an interior focus by creating a rich inner world that would reinforce the shared experience of learning to revitalize the school's academic experience.

We captured the leftover internal areaways and made them the principal architectural and experiential elements. We stripped the masonry walls and created multistory skylit spaces with shared academic programs. Inserted between the programs, full height glass walls create a sense of transparency that is spatial and adds a sense of shared experience and community. The approach here is not about architectural form, but rather about the content that enlivens spaces: transparency, space, light, color, movement, and people.

Little courtyards captured for light and learning.

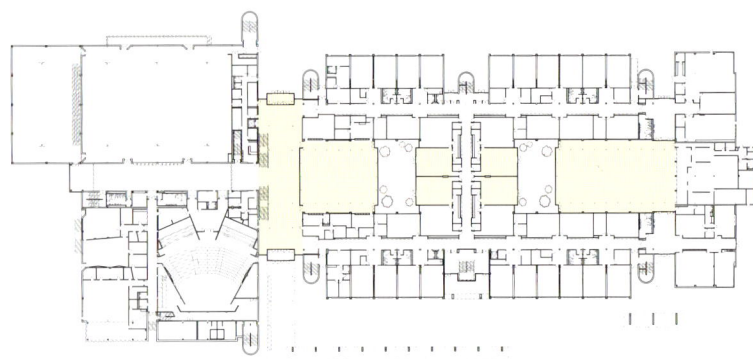

Floor plan

CHARLES R. DREW CHARTER SCHOOL, JUNIOR AND SENIOR ACADEMY

ATLANTA, GEORGIA

LOCATED ON THE "BACK NINE" OF MY favorite public golf course, the site is one of the highest points in Atlanta, with astonishing views of the city skyline. We clearly saw the design solution when we first walked the site. The site is beautiful, a rolling expanse of green with a dramatic rise along the length of the property. Placing the building at the highest point afforded the opportunity to heighten the presence of the charter school program as well as create opportunities for inspiring views of and from the building.

When a site is this rich, the response needs to be clear and straightforward. The main design gesture for the project became a sweeping arc of glass and stone, rising from the site and embracing the verdant landscape. Carefully arranged to maximize views and optimize solar orientation, horizontal shading devices are strategically placed along the curving glass wall while a row of inclined "pencil" columns supports a multistory canopy, creating an elegant porch that welcomes students, teachers, and visitors. It's a simple and powerful parti.

Now that the back nine is the school, I play the "front nine" twice.

Tilting columns accentuate the simple curve.

The solid mass of the theater
plays off the glass volume of
the classroom building.

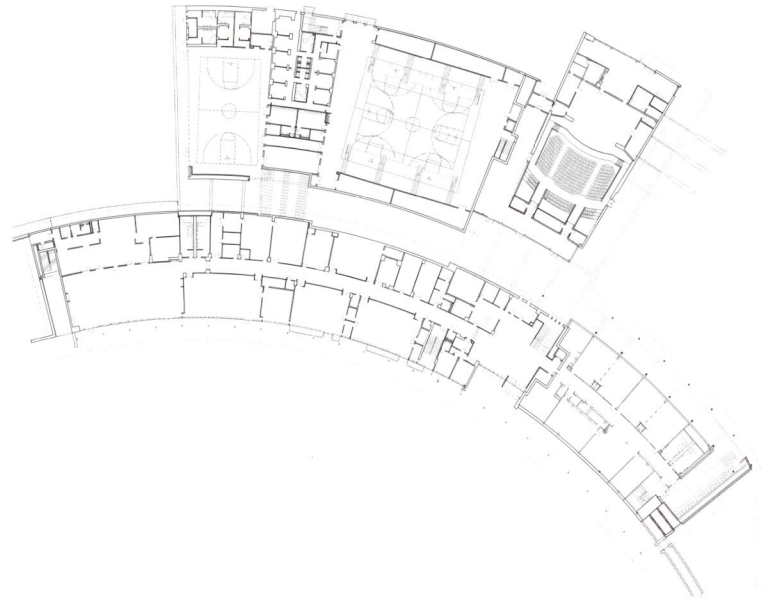

Floor plan

DRUID HILLS HIGH SCHOOL
ATLANTA, GEORGIA

THIS HIGH SCHOOL IS MY NEIGHBORHOOD school, located in the historic Druid Hills neighborhood of Atlanta. The project involved a prominent addition to a beloved 1928 historic building by Lewis E. Crook Jr. and Ernest Ivey, while connecting the various buildings that had been added on site over the years.

Our design seeks to balance the specific need to link the disconnected structures, adding much-needed classroom space with the introduction of an architecture that is modern and respectful of the prominent high school building. In deference to the original historic structure, we compositionally offset our structure in both plan and elevation, forming a gentle counterpoint that allows the existing building to be the star of the show. We developed a window pattern as a modern recall of the original building's fenestration. The garden-wall-like masonry facade of the body of the addition curves away, further emphasizing the historic structure.

Quiet, elegant, and respectful, this building, together with our Springdale Park Elementary School addition, has become a well-regarded example of modern buildings at home in historic neighborhoods.

My neighbors are happy and so am I.

The glass becomes a bridge
to the historic structure.

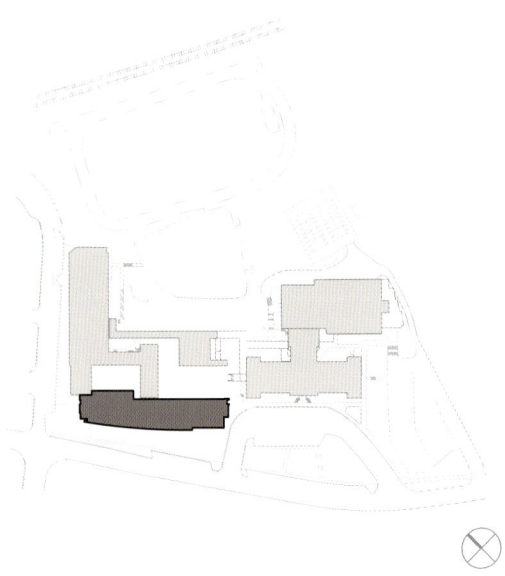

Site plan

EASTBROOK MIDDLE SCHOOL

DALTON, GEORGIA

I HAVE ALWAYS BEEN DRAWN TO
the elegance of clear architectural
compositions. Located in Dalton, Georgia,
this simple project builds on the age-old
architectural parti: the classic courtyard
building. In this case, an open courtyard
is formed by two identical academic wings
joined by a shared support wing.

The classic architectural parti contains
an innovative planning scheme that
focuses on enabling flexible, hands-on,
experiential, collaborative student work
in support of the school's project-based
learning curriculum. On each floor and in
each wing are dedicated science rooms
and classrooms that accommodate
language arts, social studies, math,
foreign language, and special education.
All of these rooms open into a large, high-
tech project lab space.

At the heart of the school is an open
courtyard and outdoor learning space.
We detailed the courtyard's facing walls
with simple glass walls that reinforce the
connection and continuity of learning from
the interior to the exterior. Simple in form,
the experience of the school is the major
architectural player, with transparency,
color, and light reinforcing learning and
collaboration.

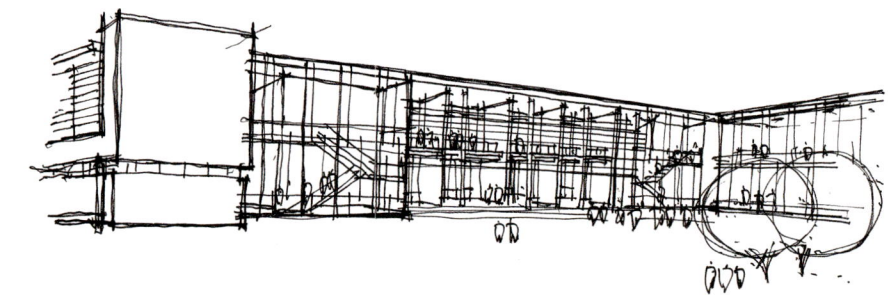

Open learning spaces inside; open courtyard outside.

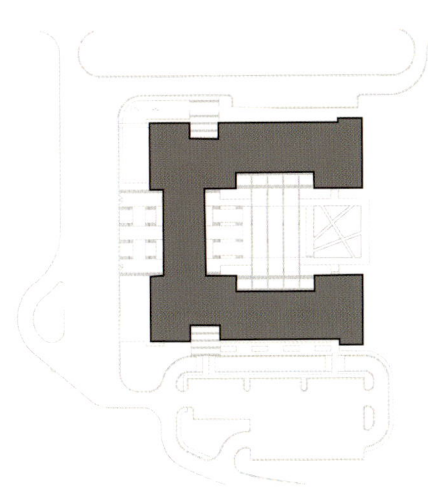

Site plan

SPRINGDALE PARK ELEMENTARY SCHOOL

ATLANTA, GEORGIA

THREE BLOCKS FROM MY HOME,
this project is located in historic Druid Hills, an Olmstead-designed neighborhood in Atlanta. The project consisted of the renovation and addition to a magnificent house by renowned neoclassical architect Neel Reid. With the historic neighborhood committee watching our every move, we designed a project that was both modern and at home with traditional architecture.

My wife, Dale, had the wonderful idea to create a carriage house structure adjacent to the historic house that would extend and establish a contextual framework for a modern building expansion. The design came quickly together and was embraced by the historic board as well as the community.

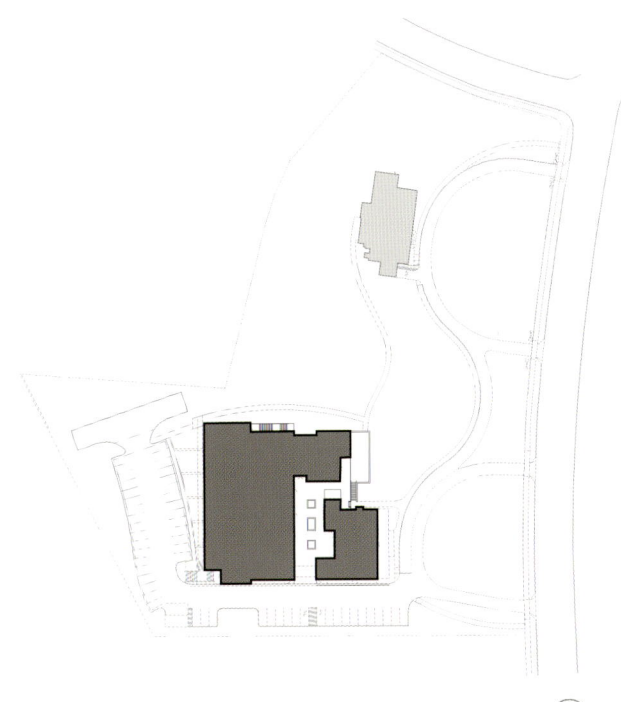

Site plan

D.M. THERRELL HIGH SCHOOL

ATLANTA, GEORGIA

ARCHITECTURE CAN MAKE A DIFFERENCE.
This project is part of the Atlanta Public Schools' transition to smaller "learning communities." In this administrative context and economically challenged district, we re-designed and repositioned an existing high school to support learning academies in an environment that is open, welcoming, and forward-looking.

Replacing the majority of the old structure, we added a new three-story classroom building between the existing gymnasium and theater, which were then renovated. We created a new media center and cafeteria at the heart of the school in order to encourage student use throughout the day. These open, transparent spaces, together with the classroom building, frame a new school commons.

As a conduit for natural daylight and views, the redesigned building is a transformative setting for Therrell High School and its community.

Sunscreens as textural articulation.

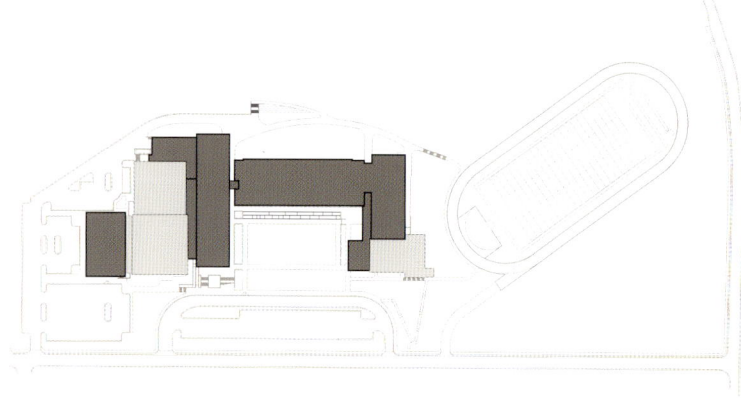

Site plan

DESIGN FOR
INNOVATION

NATIONAL INSTITUTES OF HEALTH, JOHN EDWARD PORTER NEUROSCIENCE RESEARCH CENTER

BETHESDA, MARYLAND

I FIND THAT ADDITIONS TO EXISTING buildings are both interesting and challenging. Working with an existing architectural parti demands an understanding of the ideas behind the original thought and creates the opportunity to complete that thought, enhancing the original and establishing a new whole.

This project is the completion of the Porter Neuroscience Center at the National Institutes of Health campus in Maryland. It is also an addition to the distinguished Porter Phase I building by Rafael Viñoly. Our charge was to design a building to provide broad, flexible laboratory spaces and to work with Phase I to create an innovative and collaborative community workplace for neuroscientists.

We expanded the material language and carefully worked with the regulating lines of the existing structure to create a new architectural expression responsive to the client goals and at home with the original building. A multistory, vertical commons housing brightly colored conference cubes and café becomes the major social focus of the completed center.

A silver metal and glass cubist assembly forms the distinctive image for Phase II and serves as a complement to the serrated glass fins completed in Phase I. The site is designed as a park with a gently curving pedestrian walkway that encircles both phases and leads visitors to the main entrance and central hall.

The floating base.

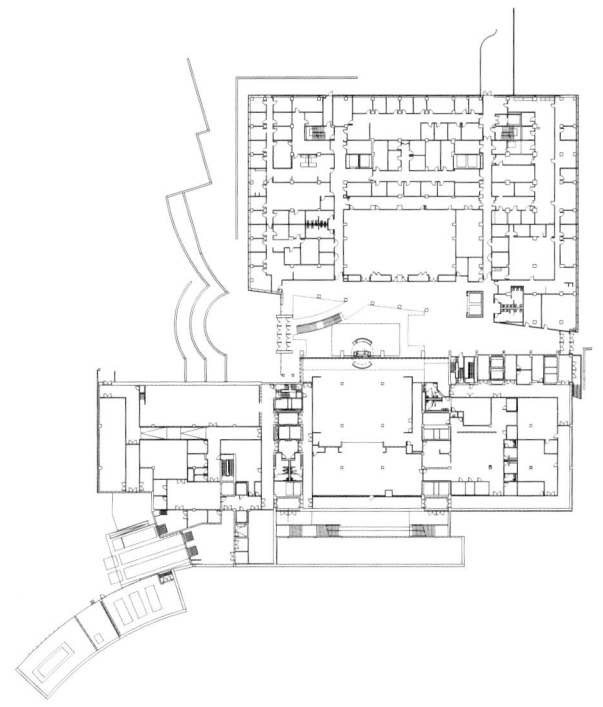

Floor plan

CENTERS FOR DISEASE CONTROL AND PREVENTION, NATIONAL CENTER FOR ENVIRONMENTAL HEALTH, BUILDING 110

ATLANTA, GEORGIA

OUR TEAM WAS PRESENTING A preliminary concept for this project, a building focused on national environmental health, at the Centers for Disease Control on September 11, 2001. The building program was significantly expanded as a result of the events of that day.

CDC 110 is a high performance building that advances the design of specialized laboratories. Designed to be rapidly and easily reconfigured to adapt to unexpected requirements, the collaborative workspaces are filled with natural light. The building expression is quiet, modern, and tailored—a serious, but supportive environment for the dedicated researchers who tirelessly work to protect our nation's health.

Daylit labs need little
artificial lighting.

Playful pattern of masonry, glass, and color.

CENTERS FOR DISEASE CONTROL AND PREVENTION, BUILDING 106

ATLANTA, GEORGIA

MY FRIENDS WHO ARE RESEARCH doctors at the CDC are dedicated, caring people who look out for the health of people around the world. When they are not traveling, many of them are at one of several CDC campuses in Atlanta. Here they do valuable research work. It's important that we make their work space purposeful, effective, and inspiring.

This project creates office space and a dining hall for these scientists and researchers. Taking advantage of a unique site overlooking a protected wetlands, we developed an architectural form that gently curves along the wooded setting. An expressive glass dining pavilion and open terraces face the tranquil view. Seen as both a workplace and a campus community center, CDC 106 quietly expresses the energy, imagination, and dedication of this remarkable organization.

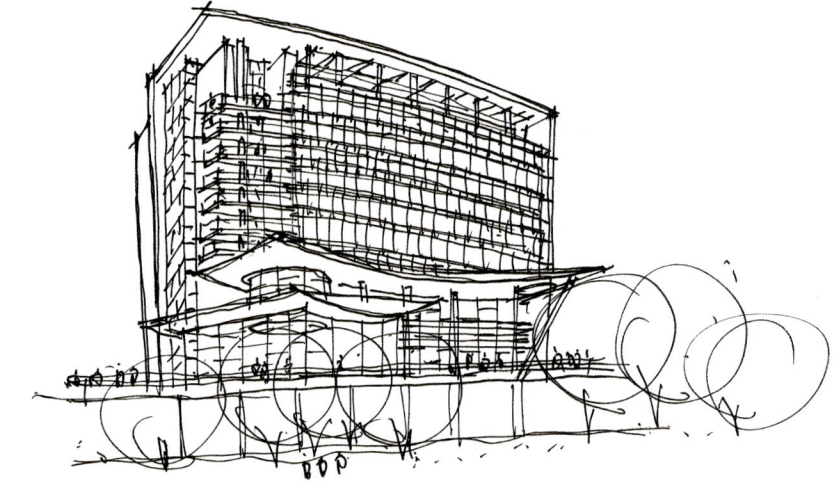

Openings to the sky.

Section

Elevated a level off the ground, the building overlooks a protected green wetland.

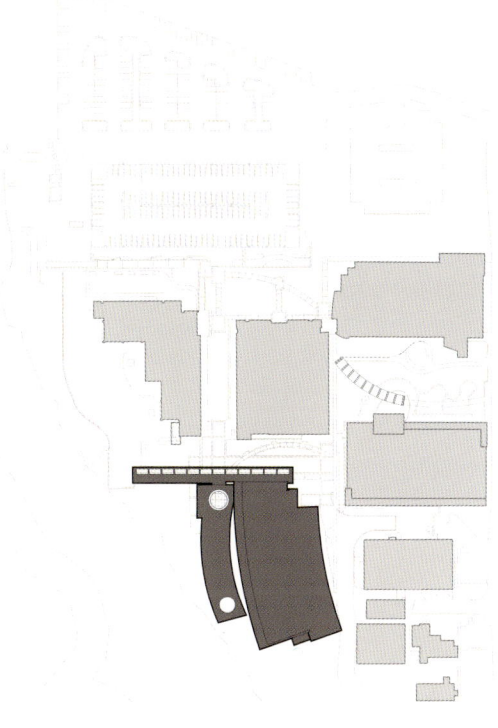

Site plan

Urban campus connections,
access to the gardens.

NATIONAL BIODEFENSE ANALYSIS AND COUNTERMEASURES CENTER

FT. DETRICK, MARYLAND

AS I ADDRESSED THIS PROJECT, I was struck by the unusual challenge of designing a building that was to be the first of its kind. Architecture is an art made up of innovation and imagination, but it is also built on precedence and context. This laboratory building, a Sensitive Compartmented Information Facility (SCIF) and bio-containment facility, has the distinction of being the first new research facility designed for the Department of Homeland Security. Due to its highly secure program, windows (major architectural design elements) are specifically in short supply.

The entry vestibule, the only major public space, includes a sculptural portal that allows secured entry into the multistory space and permits views to all office floors and controlled access to the secured building core. A glass circulation arc unites the various research areas stretching along the curving perimeter of the building and concludes at individual shared spaces. The exterior design is expressed as an elegant ship-like shape with ribbons revealing the internal movement of building occupants and nothing else.

OKLAHOMA MEDICAL RESEARCH FOUNDATION, RESEARCH TOWER

OKLAHOMA CITY, OKLAHOMA

THOUGHTS OF WIND ON THE PLAINS OF

Oklahoma inspired us to design a project that would harness the wind. We saw the building as a tower rising above its context with a clear face and strong presence. This approach would be interestingly offset by the program within the building.

The research at this facility is done at a molecular level. This very internal work can be enhanced by frequent and very often unplanned interchange of ideas among the famously introspective researchers. We were determined to compose an environment that would encourage and promote opportunities for these productive encounters.

We set up the design around a "pinwheel" floor plan concept with the laboratory spaces as the blades looking out at the Oklahoma plains and the vertical circulation and amenity spaces as the pin. Collaboration happens. The pinwheel concept is further expanded by the prominent energy producing wind turbines at the building's top. Oklahoma!

Floor plan

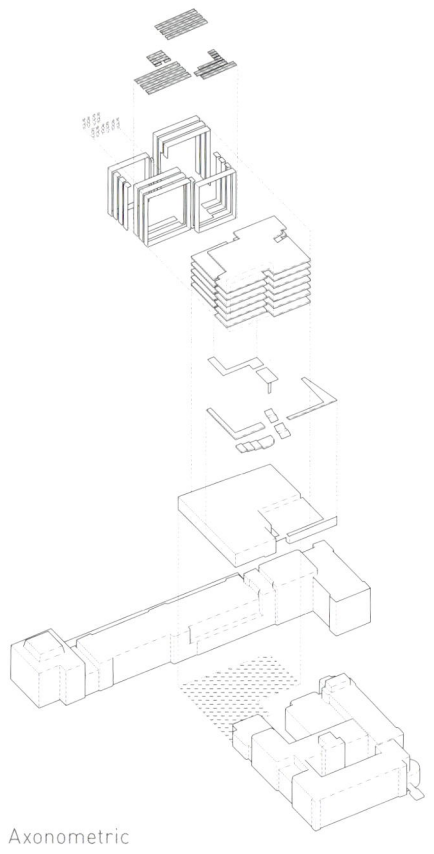

Axonometric

Turbines as
architectural devices.

CHINA HUANENG GROUP
TALENT, INNOVATION, AND ENTREPRENEURSHIP CAMPUS

BEIJING, CHINA

TECHNOLOGY AND INNOVATION PARKS are popping up on the outer rings of Beijing and other major Chinese cities. These parks are symbolic of China's innovation dream and the nation's significant progress in the global marketplace. With their muscular, daring, and forward-looking designs, these emerging campuses are the very visual and actual evidence of a national vision. They echo the massive industrial developments of the 19th and early 20th century Machine Age, but today the styles are digitally savvy, globally connected, and curiously, very Chinese.

Huaneng is China's largest state-owned energy company. Located on the outskirts of Beijing, the 31-acre site is one full block in a large, planned, innovation district. A chimera of sorts, the campus is made up of high technology research buildings, corporate headquarters office buildings, international exhibition and conference center, a 5-star hotel, plus residential blocks, and a sports center. Our approach was to design the massive program requirements as an urban park with a clear sense of connectivity between programs and between the indoor and outdoor worlds—a super block that is both a piece of the larger campus and an innovation park onto itself.

Our interdisciplinary team of architects, urban designers, interior designers, brand specialists, and landscape architects worked seamlessly to design a project that is more about place than image, more about confidence than flash, more about creating a pedestrian environment in which the whole is definitely greater than the sum of its parts. The result is an ambitious design that translates Huaneng's corporate mission into a living, breathing landscape.

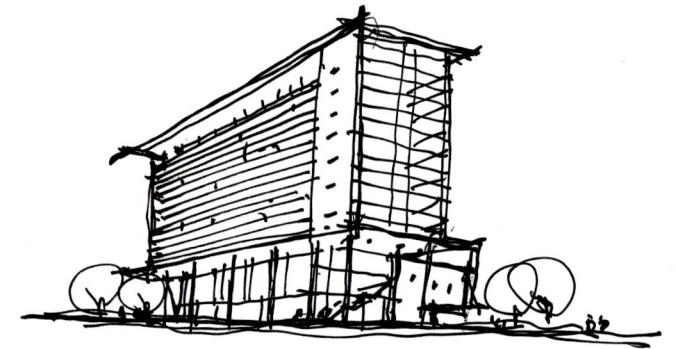

The formal entrance to a mixed-use research park.

CHINA HUANENG GROUP, TALENT, INNOVATION, AND ENTREPRENEURSHIP CAMPUS

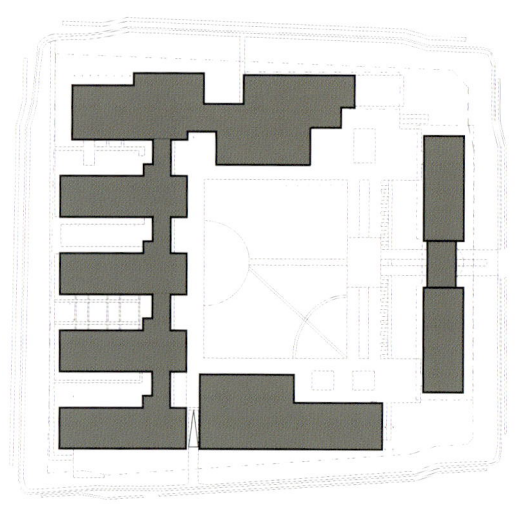

Site plan

The "floating" conference pods symbolize Huaneng's stature as the leading energy company in China.

DESIGN FOR
LIVING

EVIVA PEACHTREE

ATLANTA, GEORGIA

I SAW THIS BUILDING AS AN OPPORTUNITY to refresh the landscape of residential offerings in Atlanta. We designed the project as a vertical commons, a mini city within a city. Located in the heart of Midtown, right down the street from my office, the project responds to a growing demand for urban living in Atlanta in a way that redefines community.

The 35–story tower is made up of 392 residential units tailored for the next generation of urbanites. To stand out in the booming residential market of Midtown, we focused on best practices in sustainability, generous and varied shared communal areas, authenticity of materials, simplicity of detail, and distinctive architectural expression.

With its stacked assembly of clear cubist volumes defining retail, parking, amenity, and residential areas, Eviva Peachtree creates a bold silhouette in the Atlanta skyline. A continuous, exposed, poured-in-place brise-soleil with translucent green panels defines the building exterior, providing effective solar control. From its ground level connection to the urban fabric of Midtown to the dramatic views from the shared decks and private balconies, Eviva Peachtree offers multiple levels for people to experience the energy of this changing city.

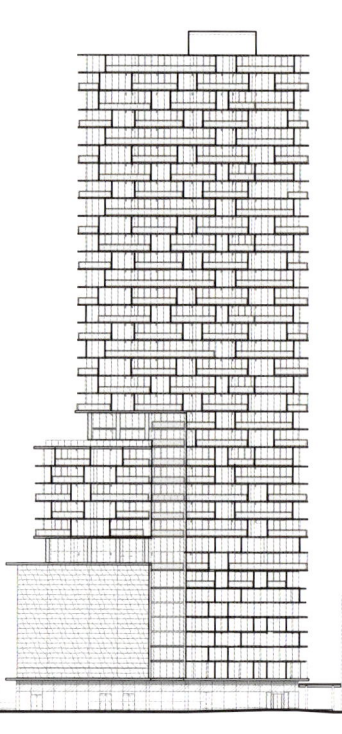

Overlapping forms denote
progression in urban scale.

TOPKAPI PLOT COMMUNITY

CONCEPT LEVEL DEVELOPMENT
ISTANBUL, TURKEY

FOR ME, TOPKAPI WAS THE NAME OF the Jules Dassin film from the early '60s starring Melina Mercouri. It involves a plot to steal a valuable art piece from Istanbul's famous Topkapi Palace. Topkapi is also the name of a transitioning industrial neighborhood in northwest Istanbul.

The average age in Istanbul is 25. This project is a response to the rising demand from a young generation for modern, integrated urban living at the heart of this historic metropolis. Here, our clients proposed to take the site of a glass factory and create a visionary mixed-use residential development.

Our team, comprising urban designers, architects, landscape architects, interior architects, and brand specialists focused on creating a real master plan, one that interprets life as a path marked by personal stages characterized by individual cultural and social preferences, and then folding a path that binds them together into a physical and compositional design for the site. The unique interests and needs of each stage drive the design.

The architecture is designed around a set of shared design elements, with common construction and materials emphasizing the streamlined private spaces and maximizing the shared spaces.

For each of the four stages, the elements are applied and customized to create four distinct projects forming four distinct environments. The unit designs are grounded in flexibility and maximize the space in the residential units with generous and imaginative shared spaces forming the essence of the design. Green space is a premium in Istanbul. In this project, green space, representing life and breath, is heightened and celebrated. Courtyards, gardens, terraces, roof gardens, retail urban plazas, and sports fields, become the central public and compositional foci and link together to create a unique, open, green development that is the heart of a revitalizing Istanbul.

I love the film and the project.

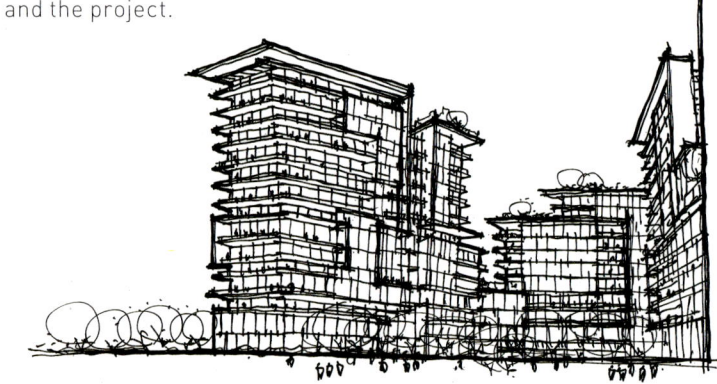

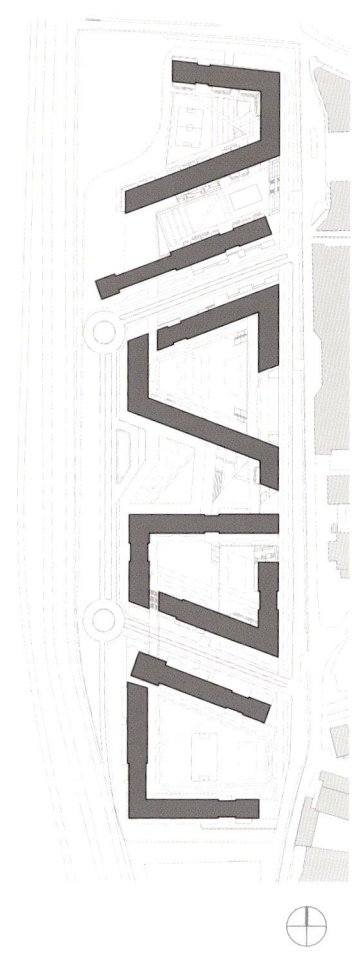

Site plan

SULTANBEYLI

ISTANBUL, TURKEY

I WALKED THE SITE ON A GREY DAY IN March. Open, unclaimed, and ready for development, the site was bordered by low-scale modest residential and retail buildings. The neighborhood needed a spark.

Sultanbeyli is a rapidly growing suburb located on the Asia side of Istanbul. The area was mostly farmland until the 1950s. The town center, which is low-key and dated, lies on the main highway between Istanbul and Ankara and includes a major public plaza.

Our project was a large-scale, mixed-use development on the site between the pedestrian plaza and the highway. We were given the challenge to create an active, forward-looking development that speaks of the energy and growth of this community.

Walking the site, we were startled to discover the pedestrian plaza. It's the kind of visionary project that is often proposed, but never built. Here it was built. Busy streets with car traffic are diverted under the plaza, establishing a walking plaza that opens onto stores that serve the community. The plaza was filled with people strolling, shopping, and enjoying themselves. Our site is an open field bordering the plaza. What an opportunity!

Our approach was to build on the connection and link to it a dynamic, vibrant, mixed-use destination to shop, work, and live. Two trellis-covered shopping streets connect the pedestrian plaza to a generous public park. A sculptural residential tower faces the park and establishes a distinctive form that becomes a bold expression of Sultanbeyli's vibrancy and growth. Revitalization in fact and in spirit. This is the kind of inspiring urban and architectural work that knits together communities and can have a powerful positive effect on improving people's lives.

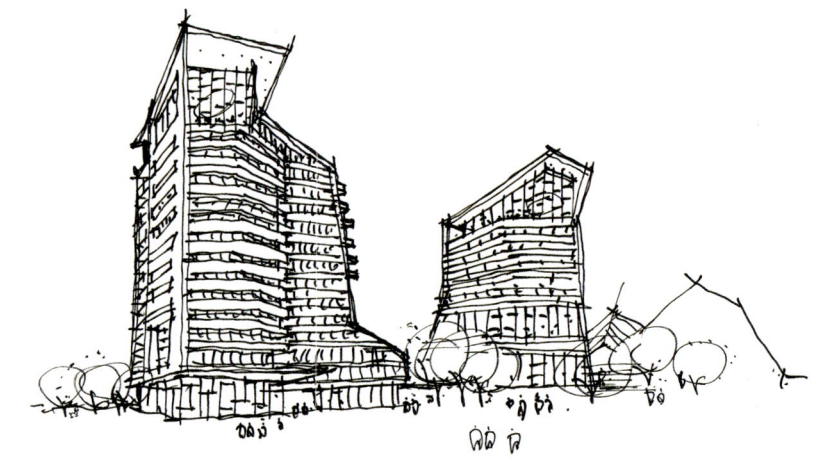

Site plan

YEDIKULE

CONCEPT LEVEL DEVELOPMENT

ISTANBUL, TURKEY

AS I STAND AT THE SEA WALLS AND look across the Sea of Marmara and down the Dardanelles, I imagine I can see ancient Troy. This is a magical place.

Located on a magnificent site on the very sea walls of Byzantium, this project is a once in a lifetime opportunity. Yedikule Station is an abandoned railroad industrial complex located within the walls of historic Istanbul facing the Sea of Marmara. The client's intent was to capture the incredibly romantic location in the shadow of the 15th century Yedikule castle to create a unique retail and hospitality destination.

On walking the site, I was overcome by a sense of responsibility. Istanbul's powerful connection to the sea has, over the centuries, influenced the growth of this timeless place and our shared culture. The ruins of once vibrant railway buildings still contained powerful and poetic qualities that would need to be incorporated into the design scheme.

Our approach was straightforward: the site was compositionally divided in plan and in section. Parking and service would occur underground, leaving the site free of vehicles.

A central opening would reveal the section and open the underground areas that would be lined with shops open to the sky. In plan, the sea-facing part of the site would feature the revitalized existing railway buildings repurposed as restaurants, retail, and cultural venues. Within the site, a sculpture garden with a sea wall promenade overlooks the Sea of Marmara. On the inland side of the site, new, modern concrete and glass buildings form a site perimeter with programs of retail and hospitality opening on the center of the development. The project is a work that integrates old and new, public and private in a historic site.

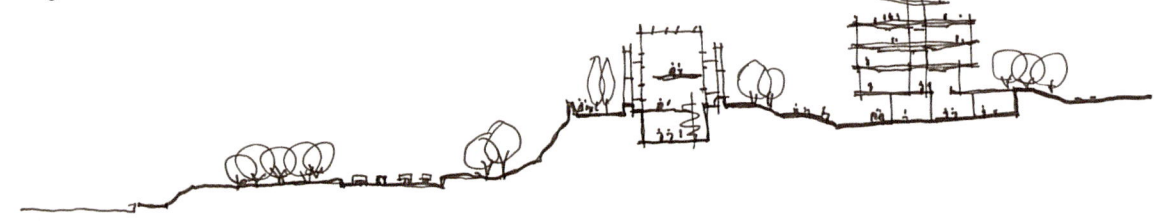

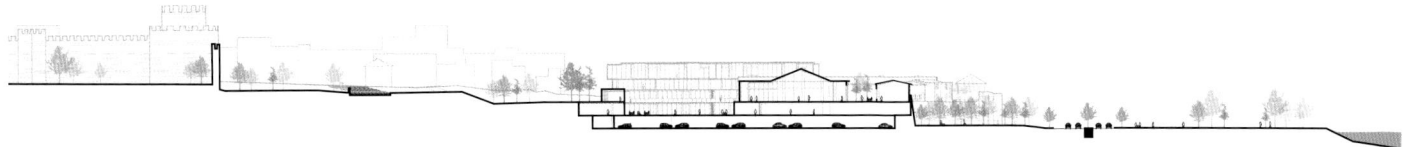

Site section

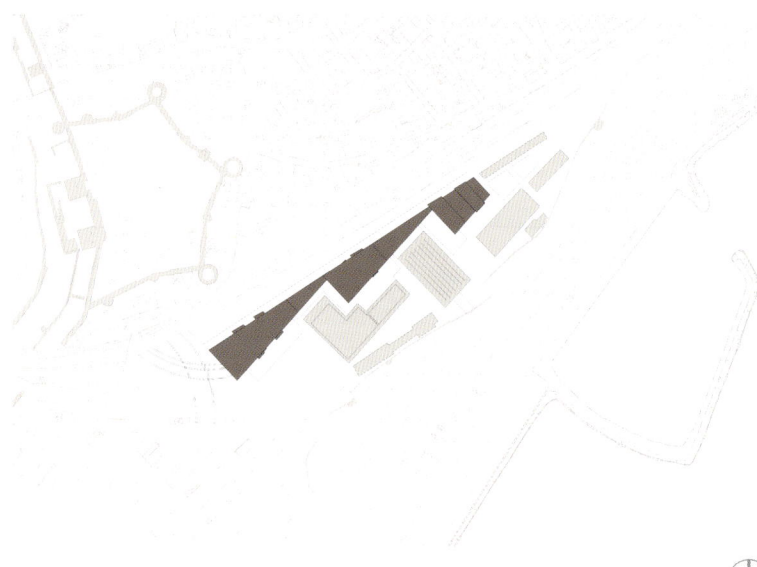

Site plan

THE TEAMS

THE ROLE OF DESIGN DIRECTOR IS LIKE A FILMMAKER.
WITHOUT THE WRITERS, ACTORS, CINEMATOGRAPHER,
AND EDITORS... I'M JUST ANOTHER GUY WITH AN IDEA.

1315 PEACHTREE STREET

ATLANTA, GEORGIA
SIZE: 45,000 SF
YEAR COMPLETED: 2009

Manuel Cadrecha, Design Director
Don Reynolds, Managing Principal
Bruce McEvoy, Project Designer

ARCHITECTURE
Peter Busby, Phil Harrison, Kim Chamness,
Katherine Duckworth, Paula McEvoy, Matt Finn,
Scott McCauley

LANDSCAPE ARCHITECTURE
Leo Alvarez, Justin Cooper, Micah Lipscomb, Zan
Stewart, John Threadgill

PLANNING + STRATEGIES
Janice Barnes

INTERIORS
Joyce Fownes, Veronica Logsdon, Ronda Miles,
Trisha Moore, David Sheehan

BRANDED ENVIRONMENTS
Eva L. Maddox, Keith Curtis, Brian Erlinder, Katie
Janson, Meredith Kinney, Brian Weatherford

STRUCTURAL ENGINEER
UZUN & CASE ENGINEERS, LLC.

MEP ENGINEER
INTEGRAL GROUP

CIVIL ENGINEER
KIMLEY-HORN & ASSOCIATES, INC.

GENERAL CONTRACTOR
BRASFIELD & GORRIE

PHOTOGRAPHY
THE MICHELLE LITVIN STUDIO (14)
RAFTERMAN PHOTOGRAPHY (13)
EDUARD HUEBER, ARCH PHOTO, INC.
(15, 16, 18, 19, 20, 21, 22, 24, 26)

BENJAMIN E. MAYS HIGH SCHOOL

ATLANTA, GEORGIA
SIZE: 360,000 SF
YEAR COMPLETED: 2011

Manuel Cadrecha, Design Principal
Barbara Crum, Managing Principal
Jack Allin, Project Designer

ARCHITECTURE / INTERIORS
Susanne Blam, Nazeer Kutty, Denise Procida,
Sumegha Shah

LANDSCAPE ARCHITECTURE
Valdis Zusmanis

STRUCTURAL ENGINEER
UZUN & CASE ENGINEERS, LLC.

MEP ENGINEER
SPURLOCK & ASSOCIATES

CIVIL ENGINEER
BREEDLOVE LAND PLANNING, INC.

GENERAL CONTRACTOR
WINTER CONSTRUCTION

CLIENT
ATLANTA PUBLIC SCHOOLS

PHOTOGRAPHY
JONATHAN HILLYER PHOTOGRAPHY, INC.

BOSPHORUS TOWER

ISTANBUL, TURKEY
SIZE: 2 ACRES

Manuel Cadrecha, Design Principal
Cagri Kanver, Managing Principal
Andrew Blocha, Project Designer

ARCHITECTURE
Adrian Bonnin, Matt Finn

URBAN DESIGN
Cassie Branum, Elizabeth Ward, Jeff
Williams

STRUCTURAL ENGINEER
UZUN & CASE ENGINEERS, LLC.

CLIENT
METAL YAPI

RENDERINGS
ATCHAIN

CENTERS FOR DISEASE CONTROL AND PREVENTION, BUILDING 106

ATLANTA, GEORGIA
SIZE: 320,000 SF
YEAR COMPLETED: 2007

Manuel Cadrecha, Design Principal
Don Reynolds, Managing Principal
David Rogers, Project Designer

ARCHITECTURE
Don Reynolds, Stephen Barefield, Kim
Chamness, Paula McEvoy, Thomas Pederson
Allen Post

INTERIORS
Cotter Christian, Grace Paul, Nicole Sheffield,
Amy Sickeler, Kim Rousseau

LANDSCAPE ARCHITECTURE
ALTAMIRA DESIGN AND COMMON SENSE,
INC.

STRUCTURAL ENGINEER
STANLEY D. LINDSEY & ASSOCIATES, LTD.

MEP ENGINEER
NEWCOMB & BOYD

CIVIL ENGINEER
URS CORPORATION

GENERAL CONTRACTOR
GILBANE BUILDING COMPANY

CLIENT
CENTERS FOR DISEASE CONTROL AND
PREVENTION

PHOTOGRAPHY
NICK MERRICK, HEDRICH BLESSING
PHOTOGRAPHERS

CENTERS FOR DISEASE CONTROL AND PREVENTION, NATIONAL CENTER FOR ENVIRONMENTAL HEALTH, BUILDING 110

ATLANTA, GEORGIA
SIZE: 145, 000 SF
YEAR COMPLETED: 2005

Manuel Cadrecha, Design Principal
Dan Watch, Managing Principal

ARCHITECTURE
Gary McNay, Ron Gill, Kimberly Pokinhorn,
Deepa Tolat

INTERIORS
Grace Paul

STRUCTURAL ENGINEER
STANLEY D. LINDSEY & ASSOCIATES, LTD.

MEP ENGINEER
NEWCOMB & BOYD

CIVIL ENGINEER
URS CORPORATION

GENERAL CONTRACTOR
GILBANE BUILDING COMPANY

CLIENT
CENTERS FOR DISEASE CONTROL AND
PREVENTION

PHOTOGRAPHY
NICK MERRICK, HEDRICH BLESSING
PHOTOGRAPHERS

CHARLES R. DREW CHARTER SCHOOL JUNIOR AND SENIOR ACADEMY

ATLANTA, GEORGIA
SIZE: 205,000 SF
YEAR COMPLETED: 2014

Manuel Cadrecha, Design Principal
Barbara Crum, Managing Principal
Chad Stacy, Project Designer
John Poelker, Project Manager

ARCHITECTURE
Andrew Blocha, Matt Finn, Neda Ghani, Joe
Jamgochian, Denise Procida, Sumegha Shah,

LANDSCAPE ARCHITECTURE
Leo Alvarez, Justin Cooper, Micah Lipscomb,
Valdis Zusmanis

INTERIORS
Neda Ghani, Marcia Knight

BRANDED ENVIRONMENTS
Keith Curtis, Buzz Busbee, Korinna Hirsch,
Christine King, Amanda McKenzie, Yancy
Wilkinson

STRUCTURAL ENGINEER
UZUN & CASE ENGINEERS, LLC

MEP ENGINEER
NEWCOMB & BOYD

CIVIL ENGINEER
PHARR ENGINEERING & ASSOCIATES, LLC

GENERAL CONTRACTOR
J.E. DUNN CONSTRUCTION

CLIENT
CHARLES R. DREW CHARTER SCHOOL
EAST LAKE FOUNDATION

PHOTOGRAPHY
JONATHAN HILLYER PHOTOGRAPHY, INC.

CHINA HUANENG GROUP, TALENT, INNOVATION, AND ENTREPRENEURSHIP CAMPUS

BEIJING, CHINA
SIZE: 2,368,060 SF
YEAR COMPLETED: 2016 ESTIMATED

Manuel Cadrecha, Design Principal
Dan Watch, Managing Principal
Bruce McEvoy, Project Designer

ARCHITECTURE
Stephen Barefield, Jane Ding, David Goldschmidt, Min Gu, Nadine Kashlan, Nadia Kulczycky, David Rogers, Marius Ronnett, Jared Serwer, Ike Tang, Eric Tsul, Ruoyu Wang, Bill Xu, Jackie Zhou, Lorraine Ziang

LANDSCAPE ARCHITECTURE
Leo Alvarez, Thomas Brown, Zhen Feng

INTERIORS
Keith Curtis, Amanda McKenzie

BRANDED ENVIRONMENTS
Keith Curtis, Amanda McKenzie

STRUCTURAL ENGINEER
BEIJING INSTITUTE OF ARCHITECTURAL DESIGN (BIAD)

MEP ENGINEER
BEIJING INSTITUTE OF ARCHITECTURAL DESIGN (BIAD)

CIVIL ENGINEER
BEIJING INSTITUTE OF ARCHITECTURAL DESIGN (BIAD)

CLIENT
CHINA HUANENG GROUP

RENDERINGS
ATCHAIN

DARDEN RESTAURANTS SUPPORT CENTER

ORLANDO, FLORIDA
SIZE: 469,000 SF
YEAR COMPLETED: 2009

Manuel Cadrecha, Design Principal
Don Reynolds, Managing Principal
Bruce McEvoy, Project Designer
Thomas Pederson, Project Manager

ARCHITECTURE
Kim Chamness, Kara Cristaldi, Ryan Dagley, Lance Galvin, Rick Harrison, Eric Lane, Paula McEvoy, Chris Sciarrone, Danny Scott,

LANDSCAPE ARCHITECTURE
Leo Alvarez, Justin Cooper, Matt Malone

INTERIORS
Joyce Fownes, Christy Cain, Meena Krenek, Veronica Logsdon, Jahae Park, Cassie Phillips, Lauren Prickett, Nancy Shea

BRANDED ENVIRONMENTS
Eileen Jones, Meredith Belafsky, Brian Erlinder, Amina Helstern, Leonard Temko, Ellen Young

STRUCTURAL ENGINEER
STANLEY D. LINDSEY & ASSOCIATES, LTD.

MEP ENGINEER
TLC ENGINEERING

CIVIL ENGINEER
MSCW, INC.

GENERAL CONTRACTOR
HARDIN CONSTRUCTION COMPANY, LLC

CLIENT
DARDEN RESTAURANTS, INC.

PHOTOGRAPHY
THE MICHELLE LITVIN STUDIO (42)
STEVE HALL, HEDRICH BLESSING PHOTOGRAPHERS (35, 36, 37, 39, 40, 41, 43-46)

D.M. THERRELL HIGH SCHOOL

ATLANTA, GEORGIA
SIZE: 240,100 SF
YEAR COMPLETED: 2011

Manuel Cadrecha, Design Principal
Barbara Crum, Managing Principal
Marco Nicotera, Project Designer
Denise Procida, Project Manager

ARCHITECTURE / INTERIORS
Susanne Blam, Jeff Chermely, Neda Ghani, Nazeer Kutty, Marc Nunes, Sumegha Shah

LANDSCAPE ARCHITECTURE
Leo Alvarez, Micah Lipscomb, Zan Stewart

STRUCTURAL ENGINEER
UZUN & CASE ENGINEERS, LLC

MEP ENGINEER
MCVEIGH & MAGNUM ENGINEERING, INC.

CIVIL ENGINEER
BREEDLOVE LAND PLANNING, INC.

GENERAL CONTRACTOR
BARTON MALOW COMPANY

CLIENT
ATLANTA PUBLIC SCHOOLS

PHOTOGRAPHY
JONATHAN HILLYER PHOTOGRAPHY, INC.

DRUID HILLS HIGH SCHOOL

ATLANTA, GEORGIA
SIZE: 140,000 SF RENOVATION / 35,000 SF NEW
YEAR COMPLETED: 2010

Manuel Cadrecha, Design Principal
Barbara Crum, Managing Principal
Marco Nicotera, Project Designer
Shawn Hamlin, Project Manager

ARCHITECTURE
Erika Morgan, Beth Del Nero, Marc Nunes

INTERIORS
David Sheehan

STRUCTURAL ENGINEER
UZUN & CASE ENGINEERS, LLC

MEP ENGINEER
JOHNSON, SPELLMAN & ASSOCIATES, INC
BARNETT CONSULTING ENGINEERS, INC.

CIVIL ENGINEER
BREEDLOVE LAND PLANNING, INC.

GENERAL CONTRACTOR
MERIT CONSTRUCTION

CLIENT
DEKALB COUNTY SCHOOL SYSTEM

PHOTOGRAPHY
JONATHAN HILLYER PHOTOGRAPHY, INC.

DUKE MEDICINE PAVILION

DURHAM, NORTH CAROLINA
SIZE: 611,000 SF
YEAR COMPLETED: 2013

Manuel Cadrecha, Design Principal
Dave Johnson, Managing Principal
Andrew Blocha, Project Designer
Bill Leggett, Project Manager

ARCHITECTURE
Jim Bynum, Ryan Dagley, Diana Davis, Joyce
Gemarino, Gary Justice, Amanda Piede, Steve
Sauer, Danny Scott, Gary Swords, Lily Wang,
Ti-hua Wen

LANDSCAPE ARCHITECTURE
Leo Alvarez, Justin Cooper, Micah Lipscomb,
Matt Malone, Alexander Stewart

HADEN-STANZIALE
LAPPAS + HAVENER

BRANDED ENVIRONMENTS
J.D. McKibben, Tom Boeman, Allison
Buskirk, Pamela Paul, Sheila Picchioni,
Lynsey Schwab

STRUCTURAL ENGINEER
WALTER P. MOORE & ASSOCIATES, INC.

MEP ENGINEER
BR+A

CIVIL ENGINEER
STEWART

GENERAL CONTRACTOR
KBR

CLIENT
DUKE UNIVERSITY HOSPITAL

PHOTOGRAPHY
ROBERT BENSON PHOTOGRAPHY

EASTBROOK MIDDLE SCHOOL

DALTON, GEORGIA
SIZE: 133,850 SF
YEAR COMPLETED: 2012

Manuel Cadrecha, Design Principal
Barbara Crum, Managing Principal
Marco Nicotera, Project Designer
Steven Brown, Project Manager

ARCHITECTURE
Neda Ghani, Joe Jamgochian, Nazeer Kutty

LANDSCAPE ARCHITECTURE
Leo Alvarez, Micah Lipscomb, Alexander
Stewart

INTERIORS
Neda Ghani

STRUCTURAL ENGINEER
UZUN & CASE ENGINEERS, INC.

MEP ENGINEER
MCVEIGH AND MAGNUM ENGINEERING, INC.

CIVIL ENGINEER
BREEDLOVE LAND PLANNING, INC.

GENERAL CONTRACTOR
M.B. KAHN CONSTRUCTION CO.

CLIENT
WHITFIELD COUNTY SCHOOLS

PHOTOGRAPHY
JONATHAN HILLYER PHOTOGRAPHY, INC.

EVIVA PEACHTREE

ATLANTA, GEORGIA
SIZE: 389,000 SF
YEAR COMPLETED: 2016 ESTIMATED

Manuel Cadrecha, Design Principal
Don Reynolds, Managing Principal
Bruce McEvoy, Project Designer

ARCHITECTURE
Tara Flache, Jonathan Massie, Mark Rahe,
David Rogers, Ti-Hua Wen

LANDSCAPE ARCHITECTURE
Leo Alvarez, Thomas Brown, Brent Pierce,
Allen Pratt

INTERIORS
Adriana Acosta, Meena Krenek, Rianna Straw

BRANDED ENVIRONMENTS
Keith Curtis, Yancy Wilkinson

STRUCTURAL ENGINEER
UZUN & CASE ENGINEERS, INC.

MEP ENGINEER
JORDAN & SKALA ENGINEERS, INC.

CIVIL ENGINEER
KIMLEY-HORN & ASSOCIATES

GENERAL CONTRACTOR
DPR HARDIN CONSTRUCTION

CLIENT
THE INTEGRAL GROUP, LLC.

RENDERINGS
ATCHAIN

GEORGIA INSTITUTE OF TECHNOLOGY, CHRISTOPHER W. KLAUS ADVANCED COMPUTING BUILDING

ATLANTA, GEORGIA
SIZE: 210,000 SF
YEAR COMPLETED: 2007

Manuel Cadrecha, Design Principal
Dan Watch, Managing Principal
David Rogers, Project Designer
Gary McNay, Project Manager

ARCHITECTURE
Lee Percy, Floyd Cline, Andrew Crenshaw,
Kimberly Polkinhorn, Mark Rahe

INTERIORS
Margaret Nysewander

LANDSCAPE ARCHITECTURE
ECOS ENVIRONMENTAL DESIGN, INC.

STRUCTURAL ENGINEER
WALTER P. MOORE & ASSOCIATES, INC.

MEP ENGINEER
NEWCOMB & BOYD

CIVIL ENGINEER
AEC INC.

GENERAL CONTRACTOR
W.G. YATES & SONS CONSTRUCTION

ASSOCIATE ARCHITECT
RICHARD + WITTSCHIEBE

CLIENT
GEORGIA INSTITUTE OF TECHNOLOGY

PHOTOGRAPHY
NICK MERRICK, HEDRICH BLESSING
PHOTOGRAPHERS

GEORGIA INSTITUTE OF TECHNOLOGY, J. ERSKINE LOVE, JR. MANUFACTURING BUILDING

ATLANTA, GEORGIA
SIZE: 151,000 SF
YEAR COMPLETED: 2000

Manuel Cadrecha, Design Principal
Gary McNay, Managing Principal
Kimberly Polkinhorn, Project Designer

ARCHITECTURE
Dan Watch, John Elvin, Karl Hirschmann,
Michael Reid, Tracy Sigmon, Bevan Suits, Bill
Viehman, Viktor Zyryanov

INTERIORS
Jennifer Glascock

LANDSCAPE ARCHITECTURE
WALLACE ROBERTS AND TODD DESIGN

STRUCTURAL ENGINEER
HARRINGTON ENGINEERS, INC.
WALTER P. MOORE & ASSOCIATES, INC.

MEP ENGINEER
NOTTINGHAM BROOK & PENNINGTON

CIVIL ENGINEER
DELON HAMPTON & ASSOCIATES

GENERAL CONTRACTOR
BEERS CONSTRUCTION COMPANY

CLIENT
GEORGIA INSTITUTE OF TECHNOLOGY

PHOTOGRAPHY
JONATHAN HILLYER PHOTOGRAPHY, INC.

MAYO CLINIC HOSPITAL

JACKSONVILLE, FLORIDA
SIZE: 850,000 SF
YEAR COMPLETED: 2008

Manuel Cadrecha, Design Principal
Dave Johnson, Managing Principal
Bruce McEvoy, Project Designer

ARCHITECTURE
Chris Borman, Diana Davis, Don Shaffer, Gary Swords

INTERIORS
Carolyn BaRoss, Diana Davis, Grace Paul, Amy Sickeler

LANDSCAPE ARCHITECTURE
PROSSER HALLOCK

STRUCTURAL ENGINEER
WALTER P. MOORE & ASSOCIATES, INC.

MEP ENGINEER
NEWCOMB & BOYD

CIVIL ENGINEER
PROSSER HALLOCK

GENERAL CONTRACTOR
ROBINS & MORTON

CLIENT
MAYO CLINIC HOSPITAL JACKSONVILLE

PHOTOGRAPHY
NICK MERRICK, HEDRICH BLESSING PHOTOGRAPHERS

NATIONAL BIODEFENSE ANALYSIS AND COUNTERMEASURES CENTER

FT. DETRICK, MARYLAND
SIZE: 160,000 SF
YEAR COMPLETED: 2008

Manuel Cadrecha, Design Principal
Dan Watch, Managing Principal
Bruce McEvoy, Project Designer
Michael Moreland, Project Manager

ARCHITECTURE
Ray Beets, Gary McNay, Alex Clinton, Pat Delmas, John Paul Dolan, Yves Gauthier, Kelly Henry, Geoffrey Maulion, Erika Morgan, Rodrigo Reyes, Mary Sabel, Deepa Tolat

INTERIORS
Cotter Christian, Grace Paul, Nicole Sheffield

STRUCTURAL ENGINEER
HAYNES WHALEY ASSOCIATES, INC.

MEP ENGINEER
AFFILIATED ENGINEERS, INC. (AEI)
CCRD PARTNERS

CIVIL ENGINEER
TRAVIS PRUITT & ASSOCIATES, INC.

GENERAL CONTRACTOR
GILBANE BUILDING COMPANY

CLIENT
U.S. DEPARTMENT OF HOMELAND SECURITY

PHOTOGRAPHY
NICK MERRICK, HEDRICH BLESSING PHOTOGRAPHERS

NATIONAL INSTITUTES OF HEALTH, JOHN EDWARD PORTER NEUROSCIENCE RESEARCH CENTER

BETHESDA, MARYLAND
SIZE: 322,000 SF
YEAR COMPLETED: 2014

Manuel Cadrecha, Design Principal
Dan Watch, Managing Principal
Bruce McEvoy, Project Designer
Mark Rahe, Project Manager

ARCHITECTURE
David Brownlee, Joe Wagner, Cathy Bunn, Andrew Crenshaw, Jeffrey Erath, Gustavo Garcia, Yves Gauthier, Kelly Henry, Rob Noma, Mark Paskanik, Mark Rahe, Renee Rodriguez, Andres Stell, Deepa Tolat, Jeffrey Welter, Angela Wooten,

INTERIORS
Tamara Cavin, David Cordell, Tama Duffy-Day, Grace Paul, Bonnie Slater

LANDSCAPE ARCHITECTURE
JORDAN HONEYMAN LANDSCAPE ARCHITECTURE

STRUCTURAL ENGINEER
CAGLEY & ASSOCIATES, INC.

MEP ENGINEER
AFFILIATED ENGINEERS, INC. (AEI)

CIVIL ENGINEER
WILLIAM H. GORDON ASSOCIATES, INC.

GENERAL CONTRACTOR
WHITING-TURNER CONTRACTING COMPANY

CLIENT
NATIONAL INSTITUTES OF HEALTH

PHOTOGRAPHY
NICK MERRICK, HEDRICH BLESSING PHOTOGRAPHERS

OKLAHOMA MEDICAL RESEARCH FOUNDATION, RESEARCH TOWER

OKLAHOMA CITY, OKLAHOMA
SIZE: 185,000 SF
YEAR COMPLETED: 2010

Manuel Cadrecha, Design Principal
Dan Watch, Managing Principal
David Rogers, Project Designer
Mark Rahe, Project Manager

ARCHITECTURE
Ernest Brackeen, Andrew Crenshaw, Yves Gauthier, Steffi Keuhnlein, Scott Sandlin, Andres Stell, Deepa Tolat

LANDSCAPE ARCHITECTURE
Leo Alvarez, Justin Cooper

INTERIORS
Cotter Christian, Cathy Jensen, Grace Paul, Christine Rule

STRUCTURAL ENGINEER
UZUN & CASE ENGINEERS, LLC

MEP ENGINEER
PHOENIX DESIGN GROUP, INC.

CIVIL ENGINEER
SMITH ROBERTS BALDISCHWILER, LLC

GENERAL CONTRACTOR
FLINTCO, INC.

CLIENT
OKLAHOMA MEDICAL RESEARCH FOUNDATION

PHOTOGRAPHY
NICK MERRICK, HEDRICH BLESSING PHOTOGRAPHERS

RICHLAND COLLEGE, SABINE HALL SCIENCE BUILDING

DALLAS, TEXAS
SIZE: 113,636 SF
YEAR COMPLETED: 2010

Manuel Cadrecha, Design Principal
Richard Miller, Managing Principal
Erika Morgan, Project Designer

ARCHITECTURE
Gary McNay, Ingrid Aboujaoude, Sean Garman, Steffi Kuehnlein, Tony Schmitz, Stacy Wyman

INTERIORS
Kristen Beighey, Grace Paul

INSTALLATION ARTIST
Larry Kirkland

LANDSCAPE ARCHITECTURE
LINDA TYLER & ASSOCIATES

STRUCTURAL ENGINEER
JASTER QUINTANILLA

MEP ENGINEER
SHAH SMITH & ASSOCIATES

CIVIL ENGINEER
JASTER QUINTANILLA

GENERAL CONTRACTOR
GILBANE BUILDING COMPANY

CLIENT
RICHLAND COLLEGE

PHOTOGRAPHY
CHARLES DAVIS SMITH - AIA

SANY AMERICA EXECUTIVE HEADQUARTERS AND ASSEMBLY PLANT

PEACHTREE CITY, GEORGIA
SIZE: 400,000 SF
YEAR COMPLETED: 2011

Manuel Cadrecha, Design Principal
Don Reynolds, Managing Principal
David Rogers, Project Designer

ARCHITECTURE
Bruce McEvoy, Stephen Barefield, Matt Finn, Ti-Hua Wen

LANDSCAPE ARCHITECTURE
Leo Alvarez, Zan Stewart

INTERIORS
Cassie Phillips, Kim Rousseau, Amy Sickeler

BRANDED ENVIRONMENTS
Keith Curtis, Yancy Wilkinson

STRUCTURAL ENGINEER
STANLEY D. LINDSEY & ASSOCIATES

MEP ENGINEER
HESM&A INC.

CIVIL ENGINEER
INTEGRATED SCIENCE AND ENGINEERING

GENERAL CONTRACTOR
HARDIN CONSTRUCTION COMPANY

CLIENT
SANY AMERICA, INC.

PHOTOGRAPHY
JIM ROOF, JIM ROOF CREATIVE, INC.

SPRINGDALE PARK ELEMENTARY SCHOOL

ATLANTA, GEORGIA
SIZE: 14,000 SF RENOVATION / 45,000 SF NEW
YEAR COMPLETED: 2009

Manuel Cadrecha, Design Principal
Barbara Crum, Managing Principal
Denise Procida, Project Designer
Erika Morgan, Project Designer
Susanna Blam, Project Manager

ARCHITECTURE / INTERIORS
Jeff Chermely, Allen Post, Marco Nicotera

LANDSCAPE ARCHITECTURE
Leo Alvarez

STRUCTURAL ENGINEER
UZUN & CASE ENGINEERS, INC.

MEP ENGINEER
SPURLOCK & ASSOCIATES, INC.

CIVIL ENGINEER
BREEDLOVE LAND PLANNING, INC.

GENERAL CONTRACTOR
BARTON MALOW COMPANY

CLIENT
ATLANTA PUBLIC SCHOOLS

PHOTOGRAPHY
JONATHAN HILLYER PHOTOGRAPHY, INC.

SULTANBEYLI

SULTANBEYLI, TURKEY
SIZE: 620,668 SF
YEAR COMPLETED: ONGOING

Manuel Cadrecha, Design Principal
Cagri Kanver, Managing Principal
Bruce McEvoy, Project Designer

ARCHITECTURE
Cassie Branum, Tara Flache, Allen Post

LANDSCAPE ARCHITECTURE
Leo Alvarez, Lauren Fraley

INTERIORS
Meena Krenek, Erika Morgan

URBAN DESIGN
Cassie Branum, Elizabeth Ward, Jeff
Williams, Yigong Zhang

BRANDED ENVIRONMENTS
Keith Curtis

ASSOCIATE ARCHITECT
DOME

CLIENT
DKY

RENDERINGS
PIXELFLAKES

TEXAS A&M UNIVERSITY, INTERDISCIPLINARY LIFE SCIENCES BUILDING

COLLEGE STATION, TEXAS
SIZE: 228,000 SF
YEAR COMPLETED: 2009

Manuel Cadrecha, Design Principal
Ray Beets, Managing Principal
David Rogers, Project Designer

ARCHITECTURE
Ed Cordes, Gary McNay, Dan Watch, Alex
Clinton, Ardis Clinton, Yves Gauthier,
Melissa Krispin, Steffi Kuehnlein, LeaAnne
Leatherwood, Mike Moreland, Stacy Robinson,
Kathy Wardle

INTERIORS
Paul Chappell

LANDSCAPE ARCHITECTURE
EDAW, INC.

STRUCTURAL ENGINEER
STRUCTURES + HAYNES WHALEY

MEP ENGINEER
SHAH SMITH & ASSOCIATES

CIVIL ENGINEER
WALTER P. MOORE & ASSOCIATES, INC.

GENERAL CONTRACTOR
JE DUNN CONSTRUCTION

CLIENT
TEXAS A&M UNIVERSITY

PHOTOGRAPHY
NICK MERRICK, HEDRICH BLESSING
PHOTOGRAPHERS

TOPKAPI

ISTANBUL, TURKEY
SIZE: 2,423,171 SF
YEAR COMPLETED: ONGOING

Manuel Cadrecha, Design Principal
David Rogers, Project Designer
Cassie Branum, Project Manager

ARCHITECTURE
Kevin Bacon, Bob Bistry, Jeff Chermely, Matt
Finn, Tara Flache, Isis Fumero, Nazeer Kutty,
Chris Loyal, Randy Maxwell, Erika Morgan,
Jared Sewer, Holden Spaht, John Stinson,
Marcy Wheeler

LANDSCAPE ARCHITECTURE
Leo Alvarez, Jason Chia, Lauren Fraley,
Patrick Soriano, Steven Velegrinis, Valdis
Zusmanis

URBAN DESIGN
David Green, Cassie Branum, Jeff Williams

INTERIORS
Isis Fumero, Meena Krenek, Erika Morgan

BRANDED ENVIRONMENTS
Keith Curtis, Marie Achterhof, Sara Allsopp,
Korinna Hirsch, Meredith Kinney

ASSOCIATE ARCHITECT
DOME

CLIENT
ISGYO
NEF

RENDERINGS
PIXELFLAKES

YEDIKULE

ISTANBUL, TURKEY
SIZE: 964,575 SF
YEAR COMPLETED: ONGOING

Manuel Cadrecha, Design Principal
David Green, Managing Principal
Bruce McEvoy, Project Designer

ARCHITECTURE
Cassie Branum, David Goldschmidt, Tenay
Gonul, David Rogers, Chris Sciarrone

URBAN DESIGN
David Green, Basak Alkan, Cassie Branum,
Elizabeth Ward, Jeff Williams

BRANDED ENVIRONMENTS
Keith Curtis, Meredith Kinney

ASSOCIATE ARCHITECT
OZGUVEN

CLIENT
EGEYAPI GROUP

RENDERINGS
HARTNESS VISION

ADDITONAL PHOTOGRAPHY
THE MICHELLE LITVIN STUDIO (4, 242, 243)
EDUARD HUEBER, ARCH PHOTO, INC. (242)

ACKNOWLEDGEMENTS

I WORK WITH EXTREMELY TALENTED PEOPLE.

In the continuum of work, I am thankful to all my partners and my teams.

In the design and production of this book, I would like to recognize the significant contributions of Deidre Mick, Hannah Palmer, Rebecca Workman, Emily Gartland, and Lauren George. I am grateful for the technical drawings created by Chris Loyal, Holden Spaht, Erika Morgan, Marcy Wheeler, and Eike Maas. I received sound critical advice from Phil Harrison, Allison Held, Eileen Jones, Cassie Branum, and Sarah Sheehy.

I HAVE AN AMAZING FAMILY.

I am completely grateful for the consistent understanding and always perceptive and honest design advice from my wife, Dale, and the unfailing support of my daughters, Christina and Susan.

MANUEL CADRECHA, AIA, LEED AP® BD+C

As a Design Director for Perkins+Will, Manuel Cadrecha's daily work is about crafting a unified design tone and orchestrating teams that elevate the possibilities for each project. Over a 35-year career, Manuel has become an ardent advocate for interdisciplinary design, driving an evolution towards a creative studio model that works across design scales and disciplines.

Manuel serves on Perkins+Will's Board of Directors and lives in Atlanta with his wife, Dale, and their two dogs.

PHIL HARRISON, FAIA, LEED AP® BD+C

Phil Harrison is the President and Chief Executive Officer of Perkins+Will. A graduate of Harvard University's Graduate School of Design, Harrison is a Fellow of the American Institute of Architects, a Senior Fellow of the Design Futures Council, and a member of the Executive Committee of the AIA Large Firm Roundtable. He serves on a number of design and arts related boards, including the National Building Museum in D.C., Museum of Design Atlanta, and the Woodruff Arts Center in Atlanta.

To learn more about Perkins+Will, visit: www.perkinswill.com

Published by: ORO Editions
Publishers of Architecture, Art, and Design
Gordon Goff: Publisher
www.oroeditions.com
info@oroeditions.com

Copyright © Perkins+Will 2015
ISBN: 978-1-941806-81-4
10 9 8 7 6 5 4 3 2 1 First Edition

Graphic Design: Hannah Palmer, Rebecca Workman
Edited by: Hannah Palmer
Production Assistance: Hannah Palmer, Rebecca Workman
Text: Manuel Cadrecha, Foreword by Phil Harrison
Project Coordinator: Deidre Mick

Color Separations and Printing: ORO Group Ltd.
Printed in China.

This book was printed and bound using a variety of sustainable manufacturing processes and materials including soy-based inks, aqueous-based varnish, VOC- and formaldehyde-free glues, and phthalate-free laminations. The text was printed using an offset sheet-fed lithographic printing process in four colors on 157gsm premium matte art paper with an off-line gloss aqueous spot varnish applied to all photographs.

ORO Editions makes a continuous effort to minimize the overall carbon footprint of its publications. As part of this goal, ORO Editions, in association with Global ReLeaf, arranges to plant trees to replace those used in the manufacturing of the paper produced for its books. Global ReLeaf is an international campaign run by American Forests, one of the world's oldest nonprofit conservation organizations. Global ReLeaf is American Forests' education and action program that helps individuals, organizations, agencies, and corporations improve the local and global environment by planting and caring for trees.

Library of Congress data available upon request.
International Distribution: www.oroeditions.com/distribution

A NOTE ON THE TYPE

The text of this book is set in Albert-Jan Pool's DIN, a modern sans-serif typeface based on the German fonts first published by the Deutsches Institut für Normung (German Institute for Standardization) in 1931. Valued for its clean, geometric lines and legibility, the DIN font family was originally designed for use in technical and industrial applications such as traffic signage. Lean, yet stylish, DIN provides a minimalist accompaniment to the diverse portfolio of work featured in this monograph.